SMALL APARTMENTS OF THE WORLD

SMALL APARTMENTS OF THE WORLD

Àlex Sánchez Vidiella

FIREFLY BOOKS

A FIREFLY BOOK

Published by Firefly Books Ltd. 2014

First printing

Publisher Cataloging-in-Publication Data (U.S.)

A CIP record for this title is available from the Library of Congress

Library and Archives Canada Cataloguing in Publication

A CIP record for this title is available from Library and Archives Canada

Published in the United States by
Firefly Books (U.S.) Inc.
P.O. Box 1338, Ellicott Station
Buffalo, New York 14205

Published in Canada by
Firefly Books Ltd.
50 Staples Avenue, Unit 1
Richmond Hill, Ontario L4B 0A7

Printed in China

Editorial coordination: Claudia Martínez Alonso
Art direction: Mireia Casanovas Soley
Text: Àlex Sánchez Vidiella, Marta Serrats, Irene Alegre
Layout: Sara Abril
Translation: textcase

XXS   XS   S

RED & BLUE HOUSES

MADRID, SPAIN

ARCHITECT // UNLUGAR
PHOTO // © ASIER RUA

To optimize space usage, a fifth floor was converted into two independent dwellings. The original height of the house and amount of natural light were regained, and the layout was made as simple as possible. The result is a main area incorporating a living room, dining room, kitchen and storage, as well as a comfortable bathroom.

XXS   XS   S

Reclaiming old wooden beams increases ceiling height and a sense of airiness, and also allows for the future creation of storage spaces.

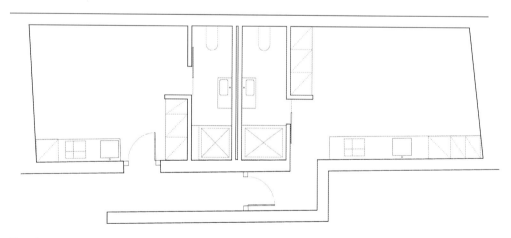

Floor plan

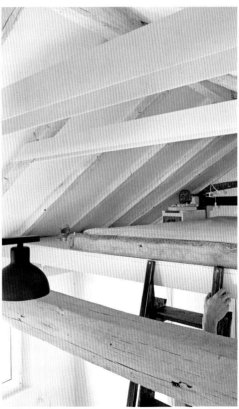

FERNANDO HOUSE

MADRID, SPAIN

ARCHITECT // STONE DESIGNS
PHOTO // © STONE DESIGNS

The renovation of this 376 sq ft (35 sq m) apartment in Madrid's historic center primarily involved changing its layout. The apartment, which was divided by a load-bearing wall, had potential as an open space and was oriented to maximize the availability of natural light.

XXS   XS   S

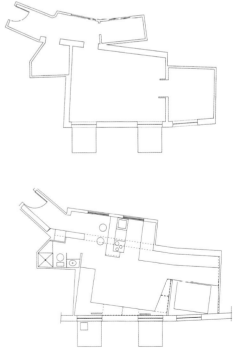

Floor plans

Low ceilings and exposed beams can overwhelm compact spaces, but painting walls white and allowing natural light to enter creates the opposite effect.

ANDRÉS BORREGO LOFT

MADRID, SPAIN

ARCHITECT // BERIOT BERNARDINI ARQUITECTOS
PHOTO // © YEN CHEN

Because the home is on the ground floor, it was possible to dig 16 in (41 cm) down into the foundation, gaining enough height to create an attic. This attic functions as a bedroom, under which are a private bathroom and kitchen.

XXS   XS   S

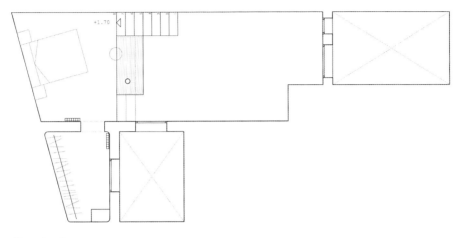

Mezzanine plan

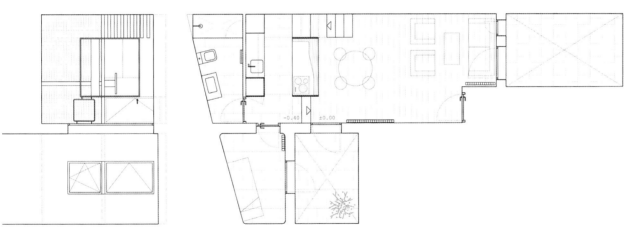

Cross section   Ground floor plan

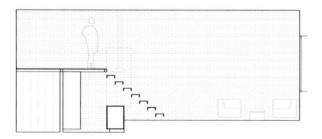

Longitudinal section 1

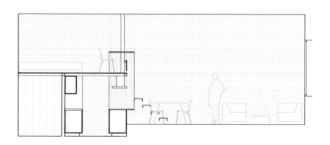

Longitudinal section 2

Using made-to-measure features, such as this 2 in (5 cm) thick laminated bar, can simultaneously provide support for an attic, a kitchen worktop and a table/balustrade.

Details

MATRYOSHKA

TURIN, ITALY

ARCHITECT // ANDREA MARCANTE, ADELAIDE TESTA/UDA ARCHITECTS
PHOTO // © CAROLA RIPAMONTI

The layout of this 430 sq ft (40 sq m) former factory is composed of various boxes, reminiscent of Russian nesting dolls. The central module, which contains the kitchen and bathroom on opposite sides, is the home's main attraction. This is an interesting and versatile feature that adds interest to the day-to-day life of its owners.

XXS   XS   S

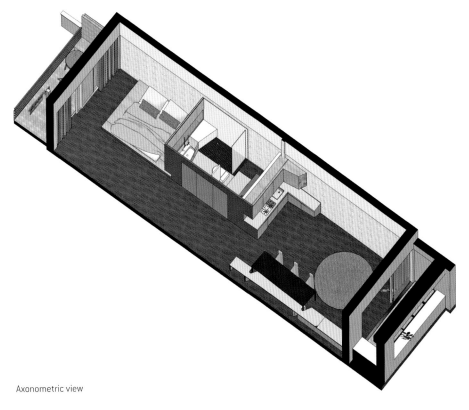

Axonometric view

FUN HOUSE

JUAN-LES-PINS, FRANCE

ARCHITECT // ANDREA MARCANTE, ADELAIDE TESTA/UDA ARCHITECTS
PHOTO // © CAROLA RIPAMONTI

In a 1960s coastal building, this apartment of just 430 sq ft (40 sq m) houses two bedrooms and a spacious main area. Inspired by the Italian communes of the twentieth century, the home is designed to be enjoyed by two families. The metal and wooden dividers generate differentiated spaces and the color scheme is nature-inspired.

XXS   XS   S

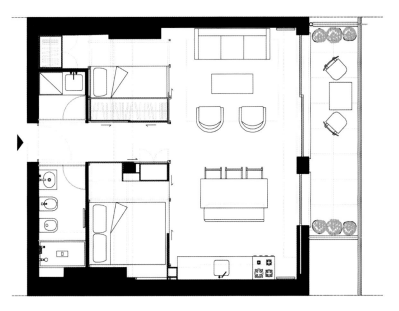

Floor plan

JEFFERSON HOUSE

SAN FRANCISCO, CA, USA

ARCHITECT // HOUSE + HOUSE ARCHITECTS
PHOTO // © DAVID DUNCAN LIVINGSTON

This project consisted of converting a space in the Marina District into a condo. The main renovations were: lowering the floor to increase the ceiling height, reworking parts of the frame in order to eliminate elements that weren't working and enlarging windows and doors. Bamboo was used as a nod to California's idyllic pastures.

XXS   XS   S

The mixture of natural maple, bamboo, rice paper, glass tiles, stainless steel and soft colors provides the desired earthy, sensual and clean look.

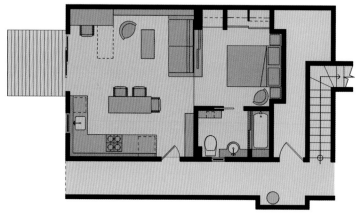

Floor plan

STUDIO APARTMENTS REYKJAVÍK

REYKJAVÍK, ICELAND

ARCHITECT // GUDMUNDUR JONSSON ARKITEKTKONTOR
PHOTO // © BRAGI THOR JOSEFSSON

This home is located in the city center, in a square in front of a church and the Museum of Sculpture. The apartment is on the second floor and has beautiful views of the surrounding area. All the spaces are designed so that you can enjoy the spectacular scenery.

XXS   XS   S

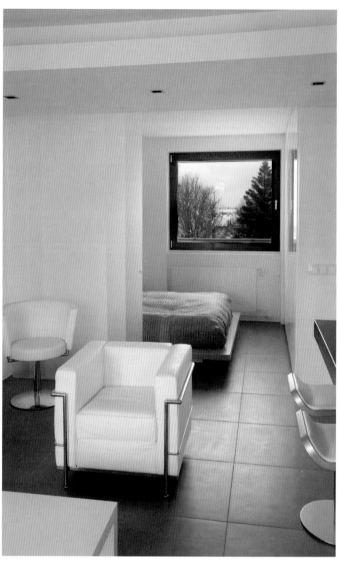

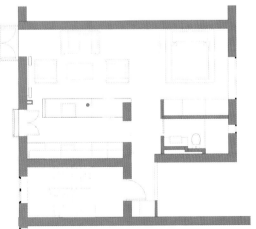

Floor plan

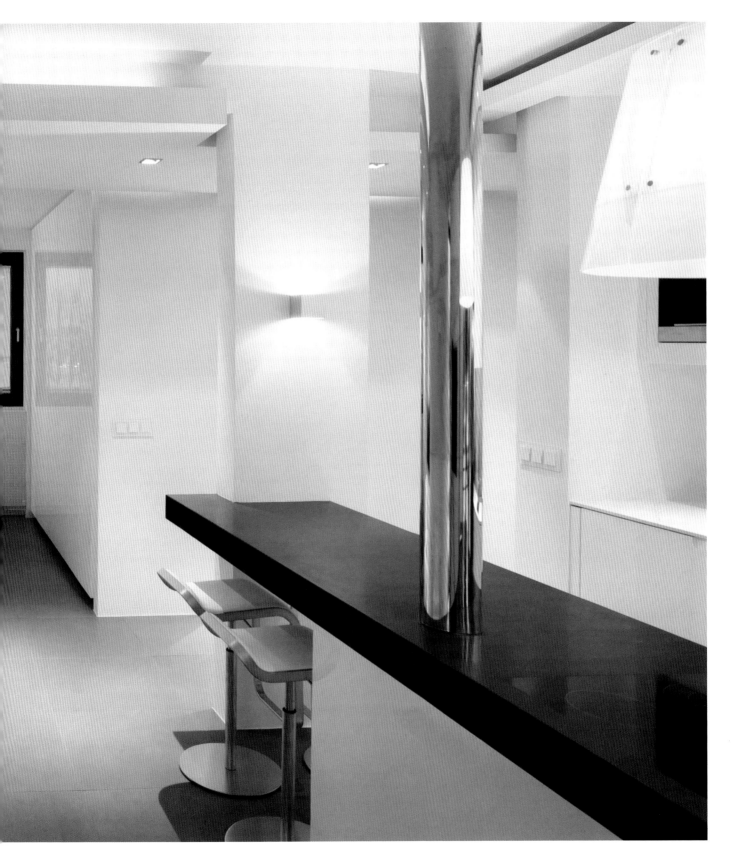

Kitchen furniture featuring white plywood is used to give a sense of spaciousness and to enhance existing natural light within the space.

If the ceiling height, as in this case, is higher than average, lights should be installed that filter and add drama to the atmosphere to create a relaxed ambience.

LARRA APARTMENT

MADRID, SPAIN

ARCHITECT // UNLUGAR
PHOTO // © ASIER RUA

In just 592 sq ft (55 sq m), a young couple wanted a place to fit in the essentials: kitchen, living room, bedroom and bathroom. The kitchen becomes the heart of the place and natural lighting is the home's star feature. The communal areas, such as the living room, kitchen and the entrance step, were designed as open and linked spaces.

XXS   XS   S

The now-classic breakfast bar, an innovative concept of American origin, is easily devised by tucking stools under the kitchen worktop.

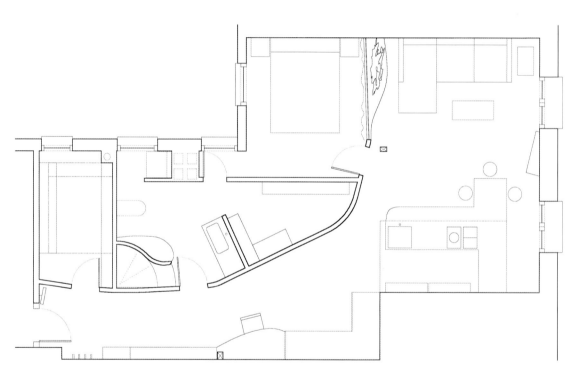

Floor plan

PRIVATE APARTMENT MM

MILAN, ITALY

ARCHITECT // TOP TAG MILANO
PHOTO // © MARCO CURATOLO

The fundamental feature that inspired this design is its 20 ft (6 m) long glass wall. The main area is designed as a single space bathed in light from the large window. A low divider demarcates the kitchen and provides storage areas at the same time. The custom furniture maximizes the use of every square foot.

XXS   XS   S

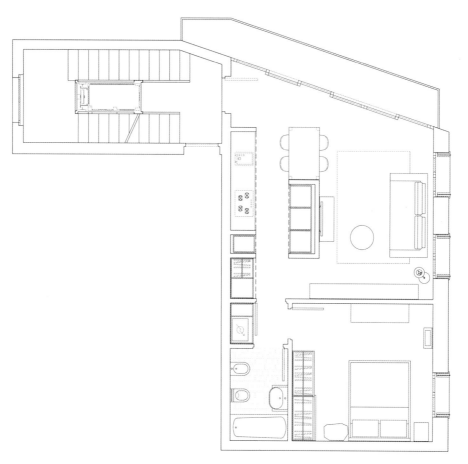

Floor plan

HOUSEWING
SEOUL, SOUTH KOREA

ARCHITECT // MINSOO LEE, KEEHYUN AHN/ANL STUDIO
PHOTO // © SUNGHWAN YOON, HEEBON KOO

Living and working areas can occupy the same space, as in this Seoul artist's renovated apartment. A dynamic, wing-like structure crosses the house, differentiating these two facets of life and maximizing the sense of space.

XXS   XS   S

Striking angular lines offer a highly contemporary minimalist look. The structure's ergonomic arrangement facilitates movement.

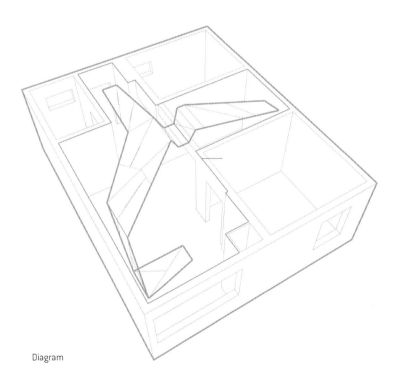

Diagram

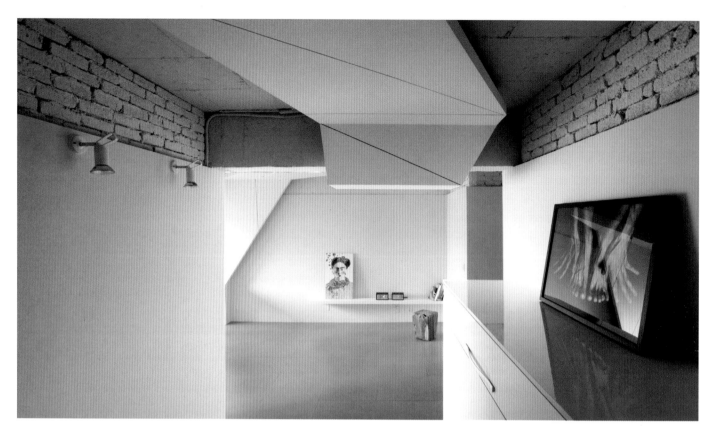

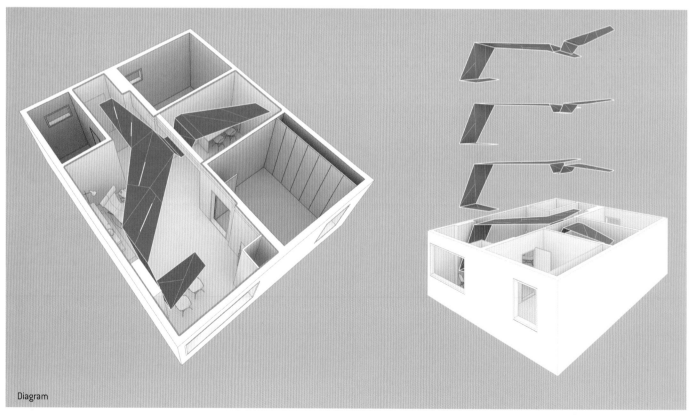

Diagram

Modular furniture is an excellent way to integrate the decor into the structure itself. This will produce a room that feels open.

ACTS
HAPPY
VALLEY
HONG KONG, CHINA

ARCHITECT // EDGE DESIGN INSTITUTE
PHOTO // © EDGE DESIGN INSTITUTE

This residential building, located in the city's historical area, houses five floors of apartments. The architects decided to use black for the design in harmony with the characteristics of the neighborhood and for the elegance conferred by this classic tonal element. The interior presents an extraordinary blend of old and new.

XXS   XS   S

Painting the ceiling silver and situating the lights strategically creates the calm and restful environment required by this apartment's owners.

The staircase banister, which echoes the whimsical style of Antoni Gaudí (though somewhat more restrained), lends the project a unique beauty.

Floor plans

AN URBAN REFUGE

BARCELONA, SPAIN

ARCHITECT // SERGI PONS
PHOTO // © ADRIÀ GOULA

At the heart of this apartment in the Eixample district of Barcelona is a room dedicated to ironing—an activity that the owner spends a lot of time on. The palette chosen ranges from the pine flooring to the yellow of the mobile objects. Decor is not necessary, because the furniture itself functions as decorative features.

XXS   XS   S

Mixing visible textures such as steel, wood and polyurethane highlights the distinguishing feature of each material.

A rotating mirror separates the bed from the bathroom behind the yellow doors.

GLAZED APARTMENT

BARCELONA, SPAIN

ARCHITECT // SERGI PONS
PHOTO // © ADRIÀ GOULA

The renovation of this apartment in the Gràcia district of Barcelona was structured around a central brick wall. This barrier divides the apartment into clearly differentiated zones (daytime and nighttime), creating visual relationships between them. As requested by the client, citrus yellow provides a cool, sharp atmosphere to the space.

XXS   XS   S

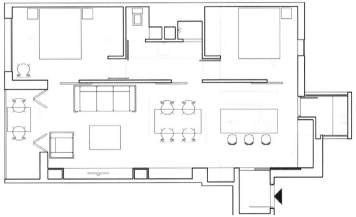

Floor plan

Choosing similar materials to outfit
a space creates a sense of unity
and harmony.

CHAMBERÍ APARTMENT

MADRID, SPAIN

ARCHITECT // JAVIER SOL GUERRERO
PHOTO // © ASIER RUA

The design objective for this 753 sq ft (70 sq m) home was to flood the space in natural light. Two small rooms and a long corridor were eliminated to create a new layout. The two adjoining lounges define the most important and prominent part of the house.

XXS   XS   S

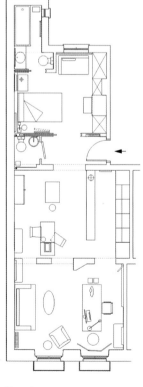

Floor plan

White walls, white floor tiles and white upholstery maximize the natural light in this home, while splashes of color bring warmth and vibrancy.

Dynamic surfaces are highlighted by the raised furniture, a clear glass table and by using the chair rail to support the art rather than hanging it from the wall.

GREG NATALE APARTMENT

DARLINGHURST, AUSTRALIA

ARCHITECT // GREG NATALE DESIGN
PHOTO // © ANSON SMART

For the sake of originality, three distinct influences are expertly mixed in Greg Natale's personal apartment: Italian art, the 1970s and contemporary design. The result was a family home with baroque style furniture, kitsch basalt flooring and Studio 54 style.

XXS   XS   S

Painting the walls and floor charcoal gray creates contrast with the white
painted ceiling and adds a theatrical touch to the home.

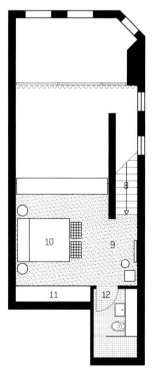

1. Entry
2. Laundry
3. Kitchen
4. Dining room
5. Sitting room
6. Terrace
7. BBQ
8. Stair
9. Dressing room
10. Bedroom
11. Closet
12. Bathroom

Floor plans

HIGH-RISE RESIDENCE
TOKYO, JAPAN

ARCHITECT // HIROYUKI TANAKA ARCHITECTS
PHOTO // © SHIMIZU KEN

The architect wanted to optimize the views of Tokyo from this apartment with
its diagonal walls. The dynamic layout and orientation are highlighted by the use
of a neutral color palette and minimalist design features and furnishings.

XXS   XS   S

Space dividers work well when they are practical and light rather than bulky.
The view from the dining room at nighttime is a breathtaking spectacle.

The central cross-shaped divider allows spatial fluidity among the three main areas: bedroom, living room and entrance hall.

RESIDENCE TSAO

TAIPEI, TAIWAN

ARCHITECT // CHUN-TA TSAO/KC DESIGN STUDIO
PHOTO // © COLA CHEN

The key feature of this Taiwanese apartment is its revolving walls, which can instantly convert four rooms into an open floor plan. The floor is dark wood and the walls are white, which ensures that the furniture stands out and reflects the character of its owners.

XXS   XS   S

Rather than the traditional divisions of enclosed rooms, the tone of a space can be made more intimate by installing a multipurpose dividing screen.

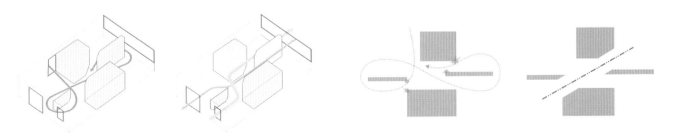

Diagram

An open floor plan, light furniture and a pale color palette impart a feeling of
spaciousness and brightness to this home.

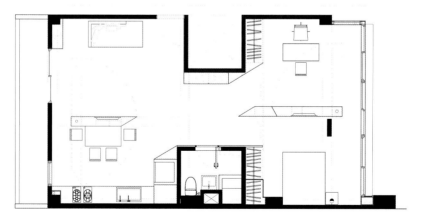

Floor plan

BROOK GREEN APARTMENT

LONDON, UNITED KINGDOM

ARCHITECT // SYBARITE ARCHITECTS
PHOTO // © SIMON COLLINS

This project entailed a top-to-bottom renovation for a family home built in the nineteenth century. The design of the 860 sq ft (80 sq m) dwelling juxtaposes old and new, showcasing the futuristic and sculptural luxury typical of contemporary architecture.

XXS   XS   S

Fresh blues and oranges create
a relaxed mood, while the use of
a variety of materials such as zinc
and quartz accentuates the feeling
of luxury.

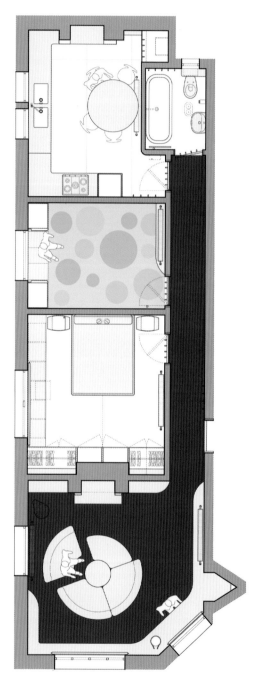

Floor plan

The bedrooms house innovative designs for organization and storage, for example under-bed storage and low furniture, all with a white lacquer finish.

MIRROR OF A FRUGAL HARMONY

ODERZO, ITALY

ARCHITECT // SIMONE MICHELI ARCHITECTURAL HERO
PHOTO // © JUERGEN EHEIM

In order to meet the owners' requirements, the architect designed large, dynamic features using a palette of whites and grays in order to provide visual and sensual stimulation. The ground floor is an open space where areas are separated by glass partitions with frosted tree branch motifs.

XXS   XS   S

An angular sofa with the back rising up to the ceiling and LED lights along its meandering shape emphasizes the theatrical atmosphere.

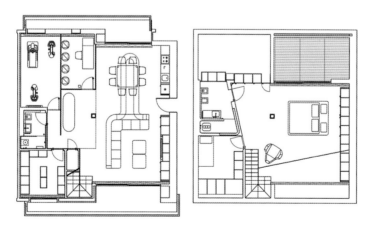

Floor plan

9TH FLOOR APARTMENT
OTTAWA, CANADA

ARCHITECT // TIM DAVIS DESIGN
PHOTO // © METROPOLIS STUDIO

For this transformation of a typical 1980s apartment, the client wanted a home that would act as a showcase for his artwork. To achieve this, small sculptures and paintings have been arranged throughout the different spaces, especially in the living room, bedroom and corridors.

XXS   XS   S

In the bedrooms, a clean and relaxed environment is created using carpeted floors, beige walls and red wine–colored furniture accompanied by subtle lighting.

ELIZABETH BAY APARTMENT

SYDNEY, AUSTRALIA

ARCHITECT // GREG NATALE DESIGN
PHOTO // © ANSON SMART

The location of the apartment meant that the architects needed to create a design focused on enjoying the views over the bay. The customer wanted a masculine design: dark oak furniture, charcoal gray stucco walls, gray stone, black basalt flooring and large windows that allow huge amounts of light to enter.

XXS   XS   S

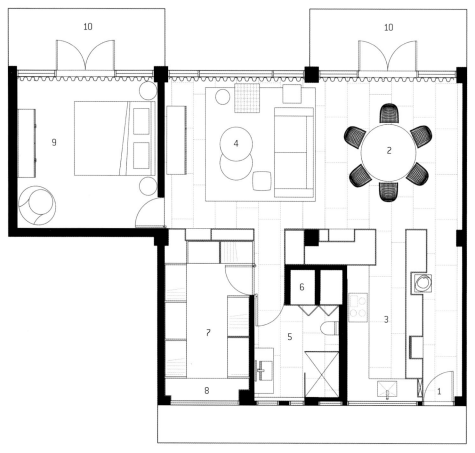

1. Entry
2. Dining room
3. Kitchen
4. Living room
5. Bathroom
6. Laundry
7. Walk-in closet
8. Desk
9. Master bedroom
10. Balconies

Floor plan

Use a combination of grays, blacks and dark purples for furniture, flooring and walls to give your apartment a masculine touch.

INDUSTRIAL LOFT
SÃO PAULO, BRAZIL

ARCHITECT // DIEGO REVOLLO
PHOTO // © ALAIN BRUGIER

This 1,076 sq ft (100 sq m) loft was designed to match its owner's personality. Modern, practical and comfortable with an industrial aesthetic, the choice of colors gives the apartment a masculine look. The kitchen and dining room are united in a single large space. On the top floor, the walls between the bathroom, dressing room and bedroom have been removed.

XXS   XS   S

LOFT
001
TORONTO, CANADA

ARCHITECT // RAD DESIGN
PHOTO // © DONNA GRIFFITH

The architects and interior designers of this 1,097 sq ft (102 sq m) loft proposed
a decorative scheme with predominantly neutral colors and striking notes
of vibrant color. Color contrast is obtained with orange cushions and red stools
and these invigorate the spaces. The kitchen is an area of transition between
cool and warm colors.

XXS   XS   S

MARKET
TORONTO, CANADA

ARCHITECT // RAD DESIGN
PHOTO // © DONNA GRIFFITH

This old 1,200 sq ft (111 sq m) warehouse was converted into a two floor loft. The design preserves the structure of the original space, with its striking wooden beams and bare brick walls, transforming it into the star feature of the dwelling. White was chosen for one wall and the kitchen to resolve the lack of light due to the small windows.

XXS   XS   S

CASA
RIZZA
VACALLO, SWITZERLAND

ARCHITECT // MATTEO INCHES/STUDIO INCHES
PHOTO // © TONATIUH AMBROSETTI, DANIELA DROZ

The interior of this four-story Swiss farm in Vacallo has been completely reconstructed to convert it into a house for the mayor. The architect highlighted the 20 in (51 cm) thickness of the old walls by the design of the windows.

XXS   XS   S

Third floor

Second floor

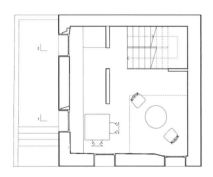

First floor

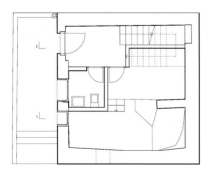

Ground floor

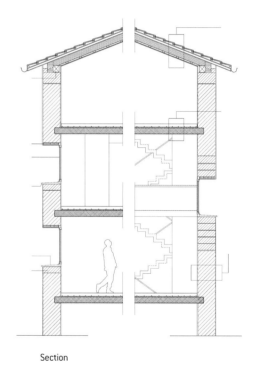

Section

JS
APARTMENT
IBIZA, SPAIN

ARCHITECT // DUE ARCHITECTURE & DESIGN
PHOTO // © DUE ARCHITECTURE & DESIGN

The renovation of a 1980s apartment required a new perspective and a change of materials to suit the needs of a young couple. Surplus interior partitions have been removed and the lack of natural light has been resolved with new materials and colors.

XXS   XS   S

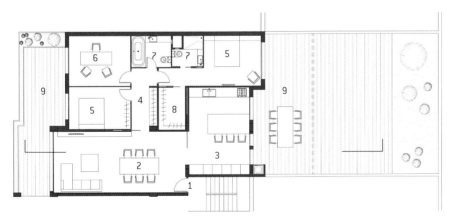

Floor plan

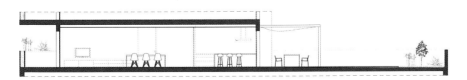

Section

1. Entry
2. Living & Dining room
3. Kitchen
4. Vestibule
5. Bedroom
6. Home office
7. Bathroom
8. Dressing room
9. Terrace

For warmth, light and a contemporary look, use light colors for flooring, walls and furniture, with a limited palette of materials and textures.

SULLIVAN APARTMENT

NEW YORK, NY, USA

ARCHITECT // SLADE ARCHITECTURE
PHOTO // © KEN HAYDEN

The main objective for the renovation of this duplex penthouse was to maximize the impact of available light and views offered by the apartment. The existing windows and interior partitions limited these features so the design goal was to create openings to capture and modulate light.

XXS   XS   S

Stone, wood, curtains and tiles are good materials to use as light receptors and, in addition to maximizing its impact, they also provide a rich array of sensory experiences.

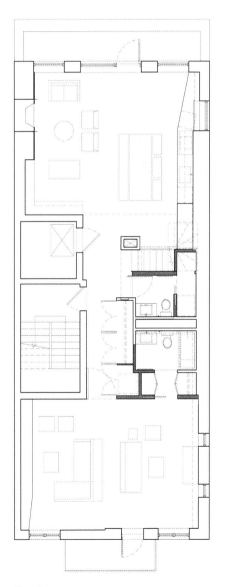

Floor plan

Using existing nooks between walls to fit in small desks or work areas is an effective and functional solution.

MIAMI APARTMENT
MIAMI, FL, USA

ARCHITECT // SLADE ARCHITECTURE
PHOTO // © KEN HAYDEN

The renovation of this apartment reflects a design suited to sporadic seasonal occupation, optimizing sea views and creating a relaxed atmosphere that is open, informal and ever changing. The existing space includes two bedrooms, a living-dining room, two bathrooms and an entrance hall.

XXS   XS   S

Using load-bearing walls and curtains to separate spaces permits a flexible and dynamic arrangement of the different areas.

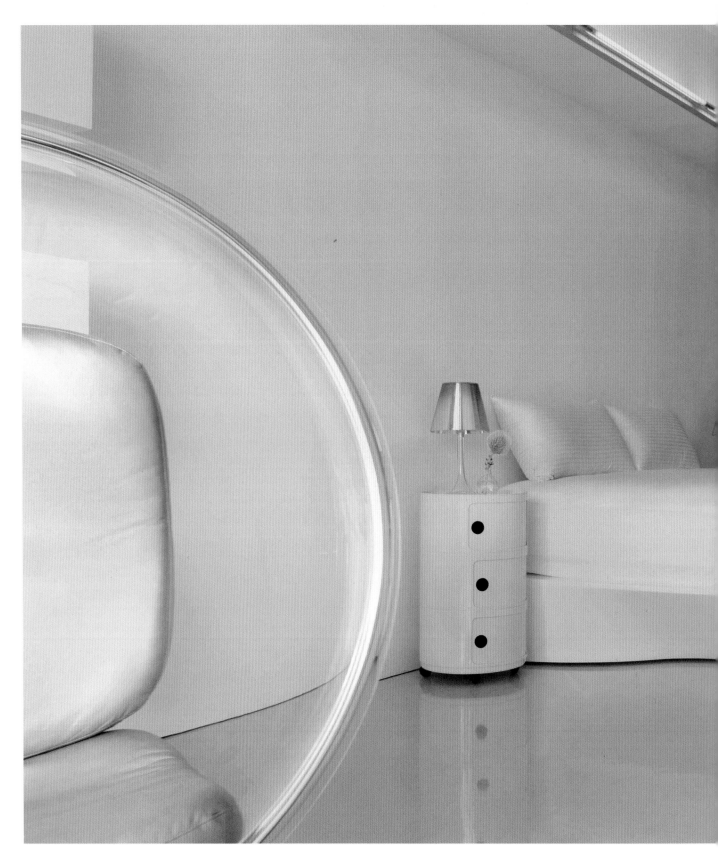

The materials and color scheme suggest an outward continuation from the inside, blurring the border between interior and exterior space.

GABRIEL MANCERA APARTMENT

MEXICO CITY, MEXICO

ARCHITECT // CENTRAL DE ARQUITECTURA
PHOTO // © LUIS GORDOA, ADAM WISEMAN, PAUL CZITROM

The facade of the apartment building was designed with the intention of building a relationship between inside and outside to connect its users to the city. The interiors of the various apartments are characterized by their flexibility and freedom to choose the layout with many possible permutations.

XXS   XS   S

To achieve a minimalist style that radiates peace and order, you must exclude any excess items and heavy decor to create a clean, pure environment.